||| || | ||||| ||| || ||||| |||
D1563419

Growing Apart

GROWING APART

LETTING GO OF OUR YOUNG ADULTS

JACK STOLTZFUS PhD

MILL CITY PRESS

Xulon Press
2301 Lucien Way #415
Maitland, FL 32751
407.339.4217
www.xulonpress.com

Unless otherwise indicated, Scripture quotations taken from
(Version(s) used)

This is the sixth in a series of books on parental practices that
help support the young adult's task of independence.

*Can You Speak Millennial "ese"? How to Understand and
Communicate with Your Young Adult*
Love to Let Go: Loving Our Kids into Adulthood
Apology: The Gift We Give Our Young Adults
*Forgiveness: The Gift We Share with Our Young Adults and
Ourselves*
*Supportive Integrity: Parenting Our Young Adults with Love and
Backbone*
Growing Apart: Letting Go of Our Young Adults

"Books are available at www.ParentsLettingGo.com and www.
Amazon.com.

Interior photos from 123rf.com

Printed in the United States of America.

ISBN-13: 9781545660065

About the Author

 Dr. Jack Stoltzfus is a licensed psychologist practicing in Shoreview, Minnesota. He received his PhD in counseling psychology from the University of Wisconsin-Madison and is a member of the American Psychological Association. The focus of his Ph.D. dissertation was on defining and measuring healthy adolescent separation from parents. His private practice focuses on parents and young adults. Dr. Stoltzfus has worked with parents and their young adult children within the context of a chemical dependency day treatment program, inpatient mental health facilities, a child guidance clinic, a youth service agency, and a private practice for more than thirty years. He has practiced family therapy as a Certified Marriage and Family Therapist and substance abuse counseling as a Licensed Alcohol and Drug Counselor. He has three grown and married young-adult children who represent the millennial and early Gen X generations.

Dr. Stoltzfus has developed and launched the website ParentsLettingGo.com to educate and support parents on practices or actions they can take to support a healthy launch of their young-adult children. Visit the website to access this book as well as the five other "practice" publications and resources.

Contents

About the Author vii

Contents. ix

Preface xi

Introduction. xiii

Chapter I Letting Go: The Final Stage of the
Launch Process 1

Chapter 2 Do Midlife Parents Have to Let Go to Grow? . . . 12

Chapter 3 Why Is Parenting a Young Adult More
Difficult These Days? 19

Chapter 4 The Situational Challenges of
Midlife Parent. 32

Chapter 5 In-laws Are Not Outlaws. 43

Chapter 6 Grandparenting: We Never Raised
Our Children Like That, and They Turned
Out Okay. 48

Chapter 7 Parents: the 24/7 ATM 58

Chapter 8 Do You Have the "Right Stuff" to Be
a Successful Midlife Parent? 63

Chapter 9 Time to Say Goodbye 66

Chapter 10 Doing Your Own Report Card 73

Chapter 11 Take Action 76

Chapter 12 Keepers. 78

Appendix A 81

Appendix B 83

Notes. 85

Bibliography. 87

Preface

A young adult leaving home can trigger a range of emotions in parents depending on the circumstances. The case of the thirty-year-old Michael Rotondo made national news in May of 2018 because his parents sought a court order to have him evicted from their house. Can you imagine the emotions these parents must have had? Saying goodbye to a member of the family, under any circumstance, is difficult. Each goodbye event, such as leaving home for college, starting a first job, living away from home, getting married, and welcoming grandchildren, reminds us that the family we created will never exist again. This book is about navigating the contraction and expansion that occurs for parents when some members leave, and new members arrive.

This book is the sixth in a series aimed at helping parents launch and let go of their young adult (see ParentsLettingGo. com). Facing the end of a family era when members start to leave can be a wrenching and devastating experience for some parents and a time of celebration for others. In most cases, it is a bittersweet event with both the joy of the graduation from the family event with the loss of the young adult and the family. I have been inspired to write this book after spending countless hours listening to parents of young adults struggling with trying to be good parents without a lot of guidance. My further inspiration is the fact that I am a father of three married young adults and eight grandchildren. This stage is different from when they were single young adults and before I became a grandfather.

As I began to explore the experience of midlife parents and their young adults, I am struck with the myriad of issues that arise for parents apart from their children as well as the complexities inherent in relationships of young adults who marry and have children of their own. This is a condensed book (no fluff) packed with quizzes to help you identify your challenges and how you are doing as a midlife parent, as well as plenty of tips, suggestions, and guidelines. You can read this in an evening and, if you're willing, you can find some key learnings to apply that can make a difference in your relationship

Introduction

"Parenthood is a never-ending journey down a wide river of worry and love. You get in the boat with your kids and you never get out. They get out—they build their own boats and row into their destinies—but you stay in the original boat, always a parent, forever caring..."

Elizabet Lesser, *Broken Open* (2015)

The End of the Family as We Know It

My wife forewarned me that our future son-in-law was going to stop by about seven o'clock to talk to me about marrying my oldest daughter. I made a note of this, but as we finished dinner, I made my way to my home office and opened my laptop only to discover that it wasn't working. Fortunately, the company I worked for at the time had IT people on twenty-four-seven, so I called in for help. What I had anticipated would take five or ten minutes was now thirty minutes, and it was past seven o'clock. There is no such thing as a quick fix to a computer problem. My wife came upstairs with a perturbed look on her face and said our future son-in-law was downstairs patiently waiting for his audience with me. I said, "Yes, I know; it will only be a few more minutes."

Somewhat closer to seven-thirty, I finally had to end the call with the IT tech. As I walked into the room downstairs, all eyes were glaring at me, and my future son-in-law popped the question—asking for my daughter's hand in marriage. He didn't seem to be perspiring too much as he asked me. I thought about the line my father-in-law said to me when I asked him for my wife's hand in marriage: "You can have her if you can afford her." But I played it straight and said, "Yes."

At that moment, it became clear to me that our family unit would never be the same again. Holidays such as Christmas, Easter, Fourth of July, and even birthday celebrations would most likely include one more. Stalling in meeting with my future son-in-law, I realized that I was avoiding this inevitable transformational moment. It represented a new stage of not only letting go of my daughter but of gaining another family member. Over time, I have had to work through the departures of my other two children and the addition of their spouses as part of our expanded family unit. And then there was the addition of grandchildren—eight as of the last count, but who's counting anymore? Initially, I resisted the plan to have the grandkids call me grandpa and suggested "Uncle Jack" but that didn't fly—more resistance to change on my part. We all outwardly celebrate these changes in the family composition but inwardly experience a twinge of sadness or grief, as we know the family we created and the special relationship we had with our children will never be the same.

Chapter 1

Letting Go: The Final Stage of the Launch Process

The dissolution of the family when children begin to leave represents both a loss and an opportunity for growth. It is no longer about growing as a family but a new era of growth apart from the family. Parents need to grow in new ways without children, and young adults need to grow in new ways without parents. How do parents let go in a way that enables growth and differentiation on the part of both parties without sacrificing the caring connection? Let me clarify the word "differentiation" as it applies to the parent and young adult relationship. To me, healthy differentiation implies separate connectedness. If, as a parent, you are separate but distant, angry, or controlling the young adult, you are not differentiated. Stick with me on this. I know the concept is difficult to grasp, but it is the essence of the healthy relationship between parents and adult children. I'm not sure that separate connectedness isn't as difficult to understand, but feel free to substitute this if it is easier to grasp.

"Differentiation" in a parent-adult child relationship is a high degree of autonomy and a high degree of connectedness or caring.[1] If both the parent and adult child are differentiated, they will be able to be autonomous, open, and honest in defining and expressing themselves while staying connected in a caring way. It is possible that a parent or an adult child might be differentiated but not the parent. For instance, an adult child has remained angry, distant, or noncommunicative and undifferentiated while the parent continues to define and express themselves in a caring way. I challenge parents in second practice book—*Love to Let Go: Loving Our Kids into Adulthood* (2017) to stay loving and pursuing of the relationship with the young adult, no matter what. This is the definition of unconditional love. When one or the other or both parties are not differentiated, each party and the relationship suffer. We are wired to connect with each other.

To move through this stage of differentiation requires at least two actions. First, it is important to embrace certain assumptions about the parent-young adult relationship. Ask yourself how much you can embrace the assumptions below. If you can't buy into these assumptions based upon reality and tested psychological principles, then you will likely struggle with both your own differentiation and that of your young adult.

Beliefs You Need to Embrace

I don't like being told I "need" to do something. In fact, I don't like being told I have to do anything. If you are like me, you may respond similarly to this statement and are prepared to argue with it. That said, I would like to ask you to think about these assumptions or beliefs and the consequences to you and your young adult if you act contrary to these. For instance, if you believe and act as if you can control an independent young adult, especially one living outside the home, I think you will be in for a struggle. Now, I'm not saying we can fully embrace all of these beliefs all of the time, but if you are suffering in your relationship with your young adult, it is likely a result of not embracing one or more of these beliefs. If you can approach your young adult with the mindset of these beliefs, you are likely to find the relationship with them on more solid ground. Check any of these that you either don't believe or have trouble following. Review your attitude and actions toward your young adult that has led to difficulties to see if the lack of subscribing to one or more of these beliefs is the underlying cause.

As a parent, I Quiz:

_____1. cannot control my young adult.

_____2. am not responsible for their decisions or actions.

_____3. am responsible for my decisions and actions.

_____4. will not use the past to excuse their actions or ours.

_____5. need to balance love (support) and emancipation (letting).

_____6. believe that relationships are inherently reciprocal—how we treat our young adult will determine how they treat us.

_____7. must step up because I can only change myself—thinking, acting, and feeling.

To this list, I would add two assumptions that are important to the final letting go stage of the parent-child relationship.

_____8. must face the loss of the family, the primary relationship we have had with the child, and face our sadness and grief.

_____9. must move forward to find personal growth through new sources of meaning, happiness, and fulfillment outside of our adult children or our grandchildren.

It's not enough to embrace these beliefs. We must strengthen specific actions or "practices" that support the healthy launch process of the young adult. Five of these practices are described in earlier books which are available through the website ParentsLettingGo.com. This final book, *Growing Apart*, addresses the need to move beyond setting limits to stepping back and focusing on life without children while maintaining a caring connection to your young adult.

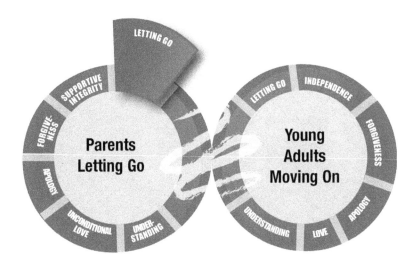

The illustration above shows a Venn Diagram in a circular model with all six practices on the left side. Unlike linear or progressive actions such as the Twelve Steps of AA, the circular arrangement signifies that we are likely to need to revisit one or more of these practices at one time or another for the rest of our parenting lives. Do we ever reach a point where we don't have to listen and try to understand our young adults? Can we show too much unconditional love? Are we likely to make mistakes in the future of our relationship with our adult children for which we may need to apologize and forgive? Will we be challenged to relate to our young adults with love but also backbone and the need to say **no** at some point in time? And finally, letting go involves grieving and saying goodbye to a relationship we once had, but also embracing a new, more differentiated relationship with our independent young adult.

PARENTAL PRACTICE QUESTIONNAIRE

To determine if you might need to revisit one or more of the first five practices, rate the extent to which the items below are true. Use the following scale:

0	1	2	3	4
Never	Rarely	Sometimes	Very Often	Always

PARENTAL PRACTICE QUESTIONNAIRE
Do you know:

____1. what your young adult likes about themselves?
____2. what they dislike about themselves?
____3. what the most difficult challenge they faced growing up was?
____4. what makes them happy?
____5. what they want to accomplish in the next five years?
____ Total

Do you:

____6. not interrupt your young adult when they are speaking?
____7. not try to fix or tell your young adult what to do, rather than seek understanding or allow them to come up with their solution?
____8. listen to understand and not to judge or direct?
____9. routinely describe what you hear your young adult saying to ensure understanding?

_____10. not allow interruptions such as phone calls, checking your cell phone, or other parties to interrupt you when you are having a dialogue with your young adult?

_____ Total

Do you:

_____11. show acceptance of their emotions without ignoring or judging?

_____12. tell them and show them that they are important and matter?

_____13. express unconditional love for them, no matter their achievements or failures?

_____14. believe your young adult can get time and attention from you?

_____15. allow them to develop their own identity and pursue their interests, needs, and dreams versus yours?

_____ Total

Do you:

_____ 16. have no regrets of actions you did or didn't do as a parent?

_____ 17. believe you didn't fail in any way as a parent?

_____ 18. not believe your parenting has contributed to the problems your young adult might be having?

_____ 19. have no desire to have a "do over" as a parent, if you could?

_____ 20. believe you have given your young adult enough time or attention when they were growing up?

_____ Total

Do you:

_____ 21. express forgiveness to your young adult or yourself without any qualifications?

_____ 22. remember the offense of your young adult without the accompanying feelings of hurt, anger, or resentment?

_____ 23. feel an emotional burden lifted through forgiveness of self or your young adult?

_____ 24. wish only goodwill and happiness for your young adult and yourself?

_____ 25. act in a more open, accepting, and caring manner since you have forgiven your young adult?

_____ Total

Do you:

_____ 26. never avoid bringing up an issue or concern because you fear your young adult's reactions?

_____ 27. not do things for your young adult that they could do for themselves?

_____ 28. not support or excuse (they were stressed, were depressed, or forgot) or otherwise tolerate irresponsible behavior?

_____ 29. never give in on a request that you know is not right?

_____ 30. never allow verbal or physical abuse?

_____ Total

GUIDE TO ANSWERS ON THE PARENTAL PRACTICE
QUESTIONNAIRE

The higher the score in any of the five question categories, the better you are doing in this practice. A perfect score of a perfect parent in any of the six categories would be 20.

_____ Items 1-5 focus on understanding your young adult. To improve on this practice, see *Can You Speak Millennial "ese"?* (2017)

_____ Items 6-10 focus on listening and connecting. To improve on this practice, see *Can You Speak Millennial "ese"?* (2017)

_____ Items 11-15 focus on communicating love. To improve this practice, see *Love to Let Go* (2017).

_____ Items 16-20 focus on apologizing and releasing guilt. To improve this practice, see *Apology: The Gift We Give Our Young Adults* (2017)

_____ Items 21-25 focus on forgiving your young adult and yourself. To improve on this practice, see *Forgiveness: The Gift We Share with Our Young Adults* (2017)

_____ Items 26-30 focus on saying no and setting limits. To improve on this practice, see *Supportive Integrity: Parenting Our Young Adults with Love and Backbone* (2018)

All books referenced above are available through ParentsLettingGo.com and Amazon.

If you feel frustrated and discouraged because of low scores on any of these practices, welcome to parenting. We're all in the same boat. Dr. David Schramm surveyed 400 empty nesters and found only 3 percent rated themselves as excellent parents.[2] Don't get hung up on the scores; instead, look for the lowest score or the practice you need to strengthen the most and pursue that. Being a parent never stops, but nor does the need for growth in these practices. Low scores are a signal that there may be some unfished work to do in your relationship with your young adult that will interfere with this last practice of letting go. For example, hanging on to hurt, anger, and resentment can keep us negatively entangled in a tense, stressful, and contentious relationship, even though we are trying to disengage. Letting go becomes more challenging when there are unresolved past or present issues. At the end of the day, we can't go back and redo our parenting, but we can commit to demonstrating these practices going forward.

The last two practices are somewhat related. *Supportive Integrity: Parenting with Love and Backbone* sets the stage for being able to let go and move on for both the parent and the young adult. Once the parent establishes a strong sense of self—who they are, what they believe, and what they will do and won't do—the young adult is forced to do the same. In this final practice, the parent's ability to move on and build a meaningful and satisfying life outside the young adult sets the young adult free to do so as well.

Chapter 2

Do Midlife Parents Have to Let Go to Grow?

B efore parents can move on and into their growth process, they need to let go of their young adults. What does this mean? It doesn't mean that you stop caring about your young adult or that you detach in the sense that you no longer want or need a relationship with them. As I have said, and others such as Daniel Seigel (*Mindsight*, 2011) have documented, we are wired for relationship, and this is particularly true of family relationships. We may say we don't need to have or continue a relationship with one of our family members, be they a young adult or sibling or parent, but our lives will be impoverished as a result. There are specific developmental tasks that midlife adults need to undertake to move toward a healthy differentiated relationship with their young adult.

Quiz

QUIZ ✔ ✔

Characteristics of a Healthy, Differentiated Parent of a Young Adult.

Take a minute to read through these and rate the extent to which these are true of you. In each case, I will briefly elaborate on the particular action or characteristic; however, we will take a deeper dive into these through the rest of the book.

The more descriptive the item is of your thoughts, actions, and feelings, the higher the score. Here is the rating scale.

0	1	2	3	4
Never	Rarely	Sometimes	Very Often	Always

_____1. Exhibit a degree of autonomy in actions and decisions. When this is present, you do not compromise your values or principles to make decisions of which your young adult will approve. You don't avoid decisions or actions because you believe your young adult would not approve. An example might be the partner you choose after a divorce or death of a spouse. You want their input but don't require their approval.

_____2. Continue to love, care, and connect to the young adult regardless of their response.
Unconditional love is just that—unconditional no matter what. You can disapprove of their decisions and actions but still love them unconditionally.

_____3. Focus on what's most important and best for you as an adult or couple.
If you are married, this is a time to turn to each other and ask the deeper questions about how you will spend the rest of your lives without having responsibilities for children. For many parents, "children come first" has been the mantra that now needs to change. If this has been true for you, now is the time to put your marriage first.

_____5. Invest in developing an adult-to-adult relationship with your young adult.
Practice listening more than talking, become a mentor to your kids, and coach and provide consultation, but let them make the decisions even if they are not in line with your thinking. As parents, we often talk about letting our kids or young adults make their own decisions, but the reality is that we are no longer in a position to "let" them make their own decisions. Let go of that thinking.

_____6. Welcome the inclusion of new family members—sons- or daughters-in-law and grandchildren. We will discuss this in the latter part of this book. It's difficult to let go of our young adults but sometimes more difficult to embrace choices they make, including their choice of a life partner.

____7. Face and resolve conflicts with one's own parents. So many unresolved conflicts or contentious relationships with elderly parents can cause stress and rob us of a time to be able to enjoy our lives. These conflicts can often become more pronounced or challenging when parents are facing illness or death. It's important to address these unresolved relationships with elderly parents to avoid these jeopardizing your time and connection with your children.

____8. Find new purposes, opportunities, and experiences to pursue without children.
Since raising children has been a dominant purpose in many parents' lives, take time to think about the second half of your life. Midlife is also a stage of life where more time becomes available for adults and couples to explore or rediscover things that they enjoyed in the past but put aside during the child rearing years. Time to pursue those ideas of what would be fun, meaningful, and challenging.

____9. Expand adult and couple friendships. Much of the positive psychology and happiness research points to the importance of relationships. This is a time to reach out to other couples, expand your activities, and build deeper friendships. These will help replace some of the emotional needs that you have met through your kids.

____10. Communicate with young-adult children in ways that respect their time, boundaries, and preferences. If they don't want you to just drop in on them, respect this. If they don't want you to be extravagant in buying presents for grandchildren and put a dollar limit on gifts, accept this. If they prefer you not call at certain times of night because this is their family time, honor this.

_____11. Demonstrating backbone in saying no to actions that would foster further dependency in your young adult. Even though young adults are working toward increasing their independence, they may still approach you for time, help, or money. You need to consider if your response will be loving, aligned with your principles, and ultimately foster greater independence. Later in this book, we will discuss specific types of contributions parents can make that meet these criteria.

_____12. Be a special person for your grandchildren. Carve out a unique role and relationship with them. Be a mentor, an advocate, and a guarantor. Don't relive your parenting vicariously. Grandparents are not a surrogate or replacement for the parents. Some parents become overbearing with grandchildren because they miss this parenting role or may be trying to assuage their guilt over their past failures as a parent. It's important not to just be another parent but to be a special person in the grandchild's life.

_____13. Strive to leave a legacy—values, gifts, learnings, etc. This is a stage when parents begin to think about what they can and want to leave to their children and grandchildren. Many parents of young adults set up a college fund or 529 for their grandchildren. Some begin to give various items of furniture or jewelry to their young adults. It's also a time, as in my family, when the young adults start to claim dibs on certain family items upon the death of the parents. "I want your coffee table when you are gone," my youngest daughter exclaimed. It's a little disturbing to hear statements like this. So I check my pulse and wonder if she knows something I don't then remind her that I'm not planning on checking out anytime soon.

_____14. Detach from feeling responsible for the young adult or responsible to fix or rescue the young adult. It's time to let go of the need to fix or make things better. It's tempting to sweep in and offer to pay for something or address some pressing need a young adult or couple might have. But one must weigh the value of the young couple's struggle to make ends meet and getting through a tough time. My wife and I were tempted to help our oldest daughter with crushing childcare costs but decided they needed to struggle through this and, in the end, experience the pride of perseverance and accomplishment.

_____15. Allow adult children to define the type of relation-ship and communication they want to have with you. Today, communication is becoming easier but more complicated. There are multiple ways in which we can stay in touch with our grown children—cell phones, texting, and email, to name a few. For others, communication may include Facebook, Snapchat, or Instagram. It's important to find out your young adult's preferred way of communicating and be willing to connect that way. Some parents have stubbornly said they will not use email or texting but, in doing so, limit contact and information. Should they come part way? Okay, maybe they should communicate to your preferred mode and you to theirs. At the end of the day, it's about staying connected however that can happen and less about whose mode is correct.

How did you do? Were there some lower scores that may suggest an opportunity to expand your healthy separation from your young adult? Consider one or more of these areas where you could choose an action that would help you be a healthier and more differentiated parent and keep this in mind when we get to the "take action" section at the end of the book.

Chapter 3

Why Is Parenting a Young Adult More Difficult These Days?

The his time of midlife and the emerging young adult is complicated for both. For the young adult facing the second period of individuation (differentiation), the first being in the toddler years, the challenges are monumental—form an identity, establish independence, build intimate, lasting relationships, find a purpose. Parents face a transformative time in their lives as well, where childrearing and the related expenses and requirements start to drop off. Oh, happy day? Not so quick to celebrate. We may face new challenges that can interfere with the successful transition into this new stage.

It is a time of risk and opportunity. It's a time of loss but also potential gain. We will discuss challenges of having to deal with slowing down and illness of both the parents and their parents. See Carter and McGoldrick (2005) for a fuller discussion of these family life cycle challenges. If you wish to read more about this, Lachman (2003) also provides a rich analysis of midlife development. Successfully navigating these troubled waters of midlife will enable you to reach a more satisfying and meaningful life both outside of and with your young adults.

Complicating Factors of Midlife

The Midlife Crisis
There's a complicating factor or force that may affect a parent's letting-go process called the midlife crisis. What is this? The Merriam-Webster Dictionary defines a midlife crisis as:

A period of emotional turmoil in middle age caused by the realization that one is no longer young and characterized especially by a strong desire for change.

There is no clinical diagnosis entitled "midlife crisis." In most cases, there is no need to run off to your physician for medication or seek out a psychologist. It generally occurs in the mid-forties, but I suspect it may be moving into the fifties simply because young adults are leaving home and getting married later. In addition, men and women work longer, and medical advances are helping with illnesses and life expectancy. Parents in the stage of midlife can often experience changes that trigger anxiety or depression. Some common changes include:

o Moving through menopause with the acceptance of the end of child bearing.

o Illness or death of a parent. One colleague said when her parent died she had this image of moving up to the edge of a cliff where her mother once stood—not a particularly comforting image.

o Change, loss of a job, or recognition that one may have plateaued in his career.
    Sometimes this can be liberating. I remember having breakfast with a 3M marketing executive who was in his late forties. He said that he had come to the realization that he was never going to be the CEO of 3M. In his case, this was somewhat freeing of the need to keep striving for recognition and promotions.

o Children leaving home triggering sadness, loss, emptiness.

o Divorce or a realization that the marriage is in trouble.

o Changes in in the body, decreased strength, and weight gain. My cardiologist informed me that one is likely to gain ten pounds between the age of forty and sixty without any change in lifestyle due to slowing metabolism—not the uplifting message I wanted to hear.

o The development of major health concerns, such as cancer or heart disease, that remind one of one's mortality and may trigger thinking about what's really important in life.

o   Finances may be affected either positively or negatively by events at midlife.

As noted earlier, most parents have to face some loss and adjustment when young-adult children are leaving the nest. If, on top of this, the parent is facing the challenges of adjusting to the aging process and struggling with their own issues of identity, meaning, purpose, and future, it can complicate the letting-go process. Such difficulties at a minimum will absorb the energy and emotions of the parent and may limit their ability to connect in a healthy way with their young adult. It may be hard for a parent to be supportive of the developmental tasks their young adult is experiencing if the parent is facing some of these same issues. On the other hand, such parents may be able to connect and empathize with the young person's challenges even though they may not be able to provide clear guidance.

The Sandwich Generation

Not unlike the "midlife crisis," another clichéé but real complicating factor in midlife is what's popularly referred to as the "Sandwich Generation" challenge. What exactly does "Sandwich Generation" mean and what are the implications for letting go of young adults? This is a generation of parents—typically boomers and GenXers—who feel responsible for children as well as their parent's health and well-being. With a young adult who has left home while others remain, the "sandwich" and pressures become more pronounced. The largest percentage of sandwich parents are between forty and seventy. If, as a parent, you have to take care of an aging parent, your time and emotional energy are severely taxed, particularly if your parent has health concerns.

Recently, I had a couple come to see me because their marriage was in trouble. They had one child out of the nest and a couple others on the runway. As we discussed the recent history of their relationship, the mother shared that she had spent the better part of two years caring for her father with cancer. As a dedicated mother, she was emotionally torn to be present with her father in his last days but also to be there for her kids. She did the best she could, but the fallout was a lack of emotional energy for her spouse. He was hurt and angry and felt emotionally abandoned because she had nothing left at the end of the day for him. Even if a parent of a young adult is not facing a health concern with one of their parents, there can be a strain on the marriage and family if the relationships with these grandparents are demanding.

The pressures of middle-aged parents are growing for a number of reasons. First, young adults are staying home longer or bouncing back and forth and continue to rely on parents for various forms of support even after they leave. The Pew Research Center has documented this trend for young adults to take longer to launch. Second, parents of these midlife couples are living longer and survive protracted illnesses due to the advances in modern medicine. This latter phenomenon can put an increased burden on parents of young adults, both financially and emotionally. In one study reported by Parker and Patten (2013)[3], 48 percent of adults provide some financial support to grown children, while one in five middle-aged parents have provided some financial assistance to a parent over the age of sixty-five. Third, there is a lot more pressure on parents, especially moms, to juggle many responsibilities. This pressure has increased as women entered the workforce and committed to careers and had to negotiate household responsibility with a spouse. Other women who suspended their careers to be home with children have invested much of their identity into raising children. Often, the women are the caretakers for elderly parents, which adds to their burden. Finally, societal and media pressures suggest parents can have it all—good parents, successful careers, health, free time, care for elderly parents, etc. So as sandwiched parents, if we are not doing all of this well, we wonder if there is something wrong. No, maybe there is something wrong with the media stereotypes and expectations, and we need some understanding and grace. Sometimes my most helpful message as a therapist is to validate the stress that these parents are feeling. "Of course you are stressed out!" Who wouldn't be?"

The Empty Nest Syndrome (Experience)

> *"In general, I find we prepare for marriage, prepare for parenting, but don't prepare at all for the empty nest. That leaves us flailing and reactionary, and that is a bad combination that results in hello, who are you and what do we do now?"*

Comment by a parent in my May 2018 survey of parents of married young adults.

A final complicating midlife factor that has a direct bearing on the letting-go process is that of the empty nest syndrome. What is the empty nest syndrome? This sounds like some type of disease. Well, in as much as it is a real experience for many parents of young adults, it does represent a "dis-ease." It is a time of discomfort due to the breakup of the family. Since I'm not inclined to label normal life events and experiences as syndromes, let's use "empty nest experience." This time in which young adults leave the nest results in a wide range of emotions from elation and relief—"I thought they would never leave"—to profound sadness and loneliness. So I want to affirm this wide range of emotions during the emptying of the nest and don't want you, as a parent, to think you have to feel a certain way.

Most parents will experience some loss when a child leaves the nest because life will change in the family. In a national survey of over one thousand parents of young adults done by Clark University in 2013, Jeffrey Arnett found that 84 percent of parents missed their kids once they moved out.[4] The change may be positive for both the family and the young adult. But if you have had a close and comfortable relationship with your young adult child and they move out or move away, you may feel like you have lost your best friend. This will be particularly true if you have been unable to effectively transition your relationship to more of an adult friendship while they were still living at home. According to Google poll of over one thousand parents of millennials, 80 percent consider their millennial son or daughter one of their best friends.[5] 55 percent of millennials consider one of their parents their best friend.[6] This finding supports the notion that parents may have a more difficult time letting go then the young adult. The more comfortable and closer the relationship, the more likely a parent will feel normal sadness and loss.

On the other hand, if the relationship has been contentious and difficult, the emotions about their leaving home may be mixed and the loss may be complicated. By complicated, I mean that you can't just have the feeling of the loss of a close friend but rather a loss compounded by a sadness of the relationship that you didn't have. There are some parallels to the experience of grief from the death of a family member or friend with whom you have not had the best relationship. I tell the story of my relationship with my father in *Love to Let Go: Loving Our Kids into Adulthood*. My relationship with my father was distant and somewhat contentious in my growing-up years. When he died suddenly in my late thirties, I experienced a sadness knowing he would no longer be available to me. The more profound sadness, however, is related to the loss of a closeness we could have had over all of those growing-up years. Whether the relationship was close or not, how can you tell if you are struggling with this empty nest experience? Since your young adult has left home, have you experienced any of the following?

_____Experience a protracted and unusual level of sadness or grief rivaling a death of a friend.

_____Continue to lose sleep or worry about your child's safety or well-being.

_____Feel rejected or abandoned when they don't contact you for an extended period of time.

_____Find that you are contacting them frequently to see how they are doing and if they need help.

_____Sense an emptiness or void as a result of a child leaving and don't seem to be able to fill this with meaningful activities or relationships.

_____Notice a tension or distance in your relationship with your spouse and can't seem to engage in meaningful conversations outside the children.

_____Experience a loss of your identity or purpose in life, which had been entirely devoted to your children.

_____Find or conjure up ways to continue to be actively involved in your young adult's life and decisions. In extreme cases, contact the college or your young adult's employer to advocate for them.

_____ Learn that friends or other family members have expressed concerns about your emotional state or your actions that suggest you have not let go of your young adult.

_____ Change your eating and sleeping habits; gain or lose weight.

NOTE: If you checked this last item, you might be experiencing some depression. In this case, please consider speaking with your doctor or consulting a therapist. Even if you don't engage in some type of ongoing treatment, it may be helpful to have a reality check with a professional. Acknowledging and facing sadness and loss are the normal grieving responses to the empty nest experience and will enable you to let go.

What Can Midlife Parents Do When Facing These Midlife Challenges?

1. Start with a physical examination to rule out both an underlying disease and to identify areas where you could improve your health. This can also reduce the fears of having some dire disease.
2. Next be honest with yourself and your young adult. Don't try to hide your struggles with one or more of these challenges. Be clear they are your issues and not theirs. They are not responsible for these issues or for fixing them.
3. Model facing your struggles and working through these with your spouse, friends, or professionals. An important message to give to your young adult is to face life's challenges and get help.
4. Try to reinvest in your marriage by being honest about your struggles and work with your spouse to brainstorm solutions. If the marriage is at risk, seek professional help. Divorce is expensive—financially and emotionally—and although it may need to happen, it's worth an effort to see if you can save your marriage. A Harley is much cheaper midlife crisis option.
5. If you are feeling symptoms of depression—fatigue, flatness, boredom, sadness, loss, or having difficulties

with sleep and eating, too much or too little of both—seek professional help. Do this before you make big decisions—leave a marriage, quit a job, or buy a van and move to Big Sur.

6. Recommit to exercise. It's a great antidepressant and can do much for your concerns with loss of strength, weight gain, fatigue, and a wide range of other problems. Consider joining an exercise program, using a personal trainer, or taking up yoga.

7. Face in to the deepest questions you have about yourself, others, and life. Get to the library or bookstore and look for books on purpose, meaning, or midlife crisis, or google the questions you have. A lot of people out there in cyberspace are wrestling with these same questions and have some ideas that might help.

8. Face out and connect with other people. It's one of the best actions you can take to reduce feelings of alienation and questions about your worth. We are wired for relationship, and we especially need this in times of crisis and change. Relationships are also a key to longevity.

9. "This too shall pass." We go through different stages in the life cycle, and no one ever just stays stuck in midlife malaise. Believe you can get through this and approach it as a growth opportunity that can enable you to move into the next stage effectively. Continually ask yourself what you are learning and make a note of this.

Growth at midlife means facing and working through these changes and challenges. Being able to let go and embrace the empty nest stage leads to growth, as does facing the "sandwich" and "midlife crisis." In Appendix A, I have conveyed the suggestions for preparing and addressing the empty nest phase of midlife from the parents in my May 2018 survey. You might appreciate their ideas.

Unfortunately, midlife parents have to face other situational challenges that involve the continuing relationship with their adult children.

Chapter 4

The Situational Challenges of the Midlife Parent

The Single Young Adult

In my survey referenced earlier, one parent summarized the problem of parenting young adults as follows:

> *"Adult children are the most difficult and frustrating to deal with because they are adults!"*

We don't give up our parenting role without a fight. This is especially true with the single young adult. Parents of single young adults often operate as if they are still in the active parenting role. The underlying mindset is, "As long as my young adult is single, they are still my responsibility." This can create a strain in the relationship because the parent may treat young adults as if they were a teenager and continue a pattern of critiquing and trying to direct their actions. This may be true even though the young adult is living away from home. The more you treat and respect your single young adult as an adult, the more likely they will act like an adult. This is a variant of assumption five described at the outset—relationships are inherently reciprocal. In this case, relationships may be complimentary with parents acting like parents and the young adult acting like an adolescent. When I was unmarried and in my mid-twenties, and my parents treated me as if I was a teenager, I reciprocated by acting like one.

Parents of single young adults often express concern about if and when their young adult will meet the right person and settle down.? Parents, we need to just relax or to use a millennial saying "just "chill out." Delaying the commitment to another in marriage gives young adults a chance to establish their identity and independence before they settle into a long-term relationship. According to the US Census Bureau, today, the average marriage age is 29.5 for males and 27.4 for females.[7] Divorce rates are tumbling, and I suspect the later marriage commitment trend may be one reason. Parents also worry about their young adult finding gainful employment and a career. Not unlike the delay in marriage, young adults are taking more time to find their niche in the work world. Millennials change jobs about every two years and don't really settle into a career until the age of thirty. They have a different mindset and expectation of choosing a job and career direction than our generation, and as such, the timing and pattern are different. They are more interested in the quality of the job and work-life balance than in the quantity of their earnings or getting ahead at any cost.

Another area of parental concern is how much financial support a parent should give to a young adult. If a young adult is struggling to find or keep a job or is underemployed and can't meet their living expenses, not to mention having a likely burden of college debt, they may turn to mom and dad for help. Parents who recognize that this is a different time for young adults and the pattern of pursuing a job or career is more irregular may be willing to help out with certain expenses and debts. Sometimes request for financial help can signal other lifestyle problems.

A couple I am seeing in counseling is deeply concerned about their young adult's lifestyle choices. Their twenty-three-year-old son is struggling with his sexual identity and making some risky decisions to seek sexual partners of both sexes in bars and through ads in local newspapers. He has reported having unprotected sex with some of these partners. Compounding this is a serious mental health problem and the use of illicit drugs. He's often threatened suicide and refuses mental health services. These parents have paid for his health insurance and inpatient and outpatient treatment but fail to see true changes in him. Parents such as these are suffering with the knowledge that their young adult is involved in risky behavior, and there is very little they can do to intervene or prevent this. It's a hopeless feeling that only parents facing this type of self-destructive behavior can understand.

You may read this and be relieved you aren't facing this situation, or you may be facing something similar and want an answer. I truly wish I could give you an answer that would force such a young person to turn his life around, but I can't. Today, we face an opiate addiction and overdose problem that is epidemic, and the largest group affected by this is this young adult population. It's excruciatingly hard to watch a young adult participate in self destructive behaviors such as dangerous drug usage. In the best of circumstances, they may admit to having a problem and even participate in a drug treatment program. Under all circumstances, parents need to continue to understand, connect, and love their young adult no matter what. In the *Parenting Our Young Adults with Love and Backbone: The Practice of Supportive Integrity (2018)*, I share certain "influence" approaches that a parent may explore, but these are always qualified by assumption one: "We cannot control our young adults." Problems with lifestyle, mental illness, and substance abuse are not confined to the single young adult. If these types of issues exist with a married young adult or couple, the challenges are exponentially more.

Parenting the Married or Partnered Young Adult

Note: I recognize that parents may have young adults who are partnered and not formally married, which has been a growing trend in our society, but I didn't want to say partnered or married young adult repeatedly. Please assume I am talking about committed partners as well as formally married couples when I refer to married young adults.

The following list of common challenges comes from a survey I conducted with twenty-five parents of married young adults, as well as other studies of midlife parents. The former was not a random sample and was done to identify challenges and solutions to parenting the married young adult. More research could clearly be done in this area. In a blog that appeared on my website, ParentsLettingGo.com, entitled *Why ParentsLettingGo.com*, I lamented the dearth of research and writing about this stage of parenting. Well, the research and writings get even more sparse when you search for information on parenting married young-adult children. Perhaps this is part of the same myth that a parent's job should be done by the time the young adult is eighteen or twenty-one, or at the very least when they are married. My argument is that you never stop being a parent, and issues continue even though your young adult is married. In fact, in some of my clients, the relationship has become more strained with the advent of a marriage.

We Have a Problem Communicating: Access, Interaction, and Communication Difficulties

In my survey discussed earlier, some parents reported that the distance between where they and their young adult lived created problems with seeing their young adult, spouse, and grandchildren. It should be noted that there is a trend for millennials to stay closer to home. Some parents have remarked that close proximity can come with its own set of problems. For instance, parents who live nearby are often expected to be available to babysit grandchildren at any time. It's a no-cost, convenient resource for which parents can feel taken for granted. The challenge for the parents is to balance their own time for work and/or retirement with time for children and grandchildren. In our case with eight grandchildren, six of whom are in town, we are conscious of not showing favoritism in providing coverage of grandchildren when needed. This plays out in the area of attending events with grandchildren—graduation from kindergarten and first grade, performances at school, and sporting events. Where did all these formal-recognition events and celebrations come from? When I was ten, I had my one only large birthday party where I could invite friends, and no grandparents attended. There are more opportunities for grandparents to be involved with their grandchildren's activities. That's a good thing but it can be challenging.

Other factors may also affect access to young adults and grandchildren. Parents in the survey reported that the young adults are so busy that it is hard for them to find the time to get together. Often, both parents are working, or one may be working two jobs, and when they have time with their kids, they are protective of this time. In some cases, the young-adult parents have put restrictions on the visits with grandchildren. This can be heartbreaking to grandparents who want to develop a deeper relationship with their grandchildren. Grandparents must respect the boundaries established by the young adult couple. Unless otherwise agreed upon, it is never a good idea to just show up at the house of your young adult or insist on having time with the grandchildren. In the end, most of these young couples begin to welcome the help and break when their kids visit the grandparents or when grandparents babysit.

Interactions with married young adults can become strained for various reasons. There may be longstanding jealousies and continued rivalries between siblings that create friction in the relationship with parents. Special events such as birthdays or holiday gatherings can be stressful and challenging. When, where, how, and who will be invited are often points of debate. The young adult couple needs to decide how they will handle these events, and parents need to respect their wishes. Our three married young adults have started a Christmas morning tradition with just their children in their own house. We are not invited, and although it seems a little empty in our house on Christmas morning, we fully support this desire to start their own traditions.

It's not uncommon for parents of young adults to complain about communication problems with their young-adult children. The toughest situation is one where the young adult has cut off communication with the parent. Sometimes the reasons for this are known, but not always. An excellent resource for this type of situation is Josh Coleman (2008). See his website: www.DrJoshuaColeman.com. Reaching out to the young adult and asking them to help you understand the reasons for their non-communication is a logical starting point. If they are able to tell you these reasons and they involve some things that were said or done by you in the past, you may have an opportunity for reconciliation. My advice would be to apologize for this past behavior without "and's," "but's," "however," or other words that are defensive and negate the apology. Even if you believe that you were innocent or correct, the goal is reconciliation and not proving who was right or wrong.

Too many families I see have become estranged because they have made the need to be right more important than the relationship. Don't let pride stand in the way of a relationship with your young adult. Take the high road; it's less crowded. Apologize and indicate how you will work on changing in the future and avoid the behavior that had created the problem. For help with the way to apologize and to avoid certain mistakes when doing this, please see practice book three, *Apology: The Gift We Give Our Young Adults.* Even when parents and young adults are communicating, there can be challenges.

Sometimes conversations between parents and young adult children are strained. In these cases, it is essential to understand the contributing factors. Being forthright and having a candid conversation about why it is difficult to communicate is a start. Take the lead in this regard and ask for feedback regarding ways you could do better in conversations with the young adult. Sometimes asking for two or three suggestions about how you could be better at conversing with the young adult is helpful. Hopefully, your young adult would reciprocate by asking how they could do better in discussions with you. The first practice book, *Do You Speak Millennial "ese" (2017)? How to Understand and Communicate with Your Young Adult,* would be a useful primer to help you think through ways to be more effective in your communications.

Some parents with whom I have worked report that their young adult can be demanding and abusive at times. This may center around help, money, or other resources to which they feel entitled. These are tough conversations, but parents need to be clear on what they will and won't do for the young adult. Being inconsistent as a parent or inconsistency between parents in approach to the young adult will only invite more demands from the young adult and efforts to play one parent against the other. Yes, this divide-and-conquer game that children learn at an early age continues well into the young-adult years. As such, parents need to collaborate and put forth a consistent message of the level of support they are willing to give. If parents are divorced, presenting a united front may be difficult, but an effort should be made to do so.

I am struck with how difficult and uncomfortable it is for parents to bring up areas of concern with their young-adult couple. At the risk of being overly simplistic, I would use the following process and example to get the best response and outcome. This is based upon an approach that engages them as partners in search of solutions versus blaming them. They will be less defensive and more willing to seek some solutions jointly. You have to be open to solutions they may come up with that are different than the ones you offered. The final solution may be a tradeoff or compromise. But again, remember you can't control your young-adult couple. That said, you are responsible for communicating respectfully and openly. Here are recommended steps to follow.

1. Start with, "I'd like to bring up a problem and ask for your help in coming up with some solutions."
2. Start your problem description with "I," not "you," which puts one receiver on the defensive. Describe the situation or concern you have and the effect on you in a non-blaming or accusatory language.
3. Indicate how you feel as a result of the situation or how it affects you. Don't say, "You made me feel…" as tempting as that can be. You can say, "I feel hurt, frustrated, etc., when… (the situation)."
4. Offer a suggestion or two as to how to address or solve the problem.

5. Invite your young adult to offer any suggestions they might have.

Here's an example of using these steps:

A parent and young adult daughter-in-law are out shopping with young grandchildren. While they are walking around, the daughter is talking or texting and expecting her mother-in-law to watch or corral the children. The mother-in-law speaks up.

> "I need to bring up a problem and ask for your help in coming up with solutions. It's upsetting to me when we are out shopping, and you spend large amounts of this time texting or talking on the phone. I am frustrated because it appears you expect me to watch the children during these times, and we spend very little time talking with each other. Would you please consider not making calls or texting when we are out? Also, if you get a call, indicate that you will call back later because you are shopping with your mother-in-law. Do you have any other ideas or suggestions as to how to make this time of shopping work better for both of us?"

Chapter 5

In-Laws Are Not Outlaws

In my recent study, one of the biggest challenges parents reported was how to relate to the spouse of your young adult. A young adult's spouse may be reserved, difficult to communicate with, and controlling of access to and time with the parent's son or daughter or grandchildren. The dilemma is how to support the marriage and their own adult child while trying to engage the spouse positively. According to Madeleine Fugere, the reasons why there may be difficulties between mothers-in-law and daughters-in-law may have evolutionary roots.[8] Although there are clearly issues between mothers-in-law and sons-in-law, in my private practice, I have seen many more of the former. In the article referenced above, Fugere reported that mothers rate the relationships with sons-in-law more favorably than those with daughters-in-law. Dr. Teri Apter, in her research over twenty years, found that 75 percent of couples reported having problems with in-laws, but only 15 percent of mother-in-law/son-in-law relationships were described as tense. She found that 60 percent of women admitted that their relationship with their female in-law caused them long-term unhappiness and stress.[9] In either case, these strained relationships lead to conflict and frustration. What are some of the underlying causes of the tension between mothers-in-law and daughters-in-law?

1. The daughter-in-law or son-in-law now becomes number one and replaces the parent. Facing this reality is critical for the parents to be able to shift into a secondary position and support the marriage and not just their son or daughter. One of the best things parents can say to a son or daughter who might disclose some problems with their spouse is to ask, "Have you discussed this with your spouse? If not, you need to, and if you can't work it out, get some professional help."

   My parents made a very conscious effort to shift from the primary relationship they had with me before I was married to a secondary relationship. Somewhat symbolically, my mother happened to be helping me with my cufflinks at the back of the church on my wedding day and said, in front of my soon to be wife, "This is the last time I will be doing something like this for you." From that point on and throughout our marriage, my parents treated and supported us primarily as a couple. They clearly stepped back and assumed a secondary role and never took sides if issues arose between my wife and me. This has been a True gift to us in our marriage. Author's note

2. Mothers-in-law and daughters-in-law have similar lead roles in the household. In most cases, mothers-in-laws may believe that they have, by experience and age, more expertise around such areas as decorating the house, cleaning, cooking, caring for children, etc. Clearly, each generation seems to come up with a new or different twist on these subjects. Boomers grew up with Dr. Spock, but mothers today have been heavily influenced by more recent writings related to attachment, organic foods, and safety practices.

3. There are a variety of other differences that can contribute to distance and strain in the relationship with a son- or daughter-in-law and may include different values, religious orientations, childrearing practices, lifestyle decisions, management of money, etc.

It would be impossible to address all of the different situations and challenges that occur relative to in-laws in this short book, but here are some guiding principles:

1. Avoid triangles where you develop secrets with one of the young adults and leave the other out. This can be especially damaging if secrets are kept from the spouse of the young adult and if that spouse is the daughter-in-law. As much as possible, communicate directly with the in-law. Don't ask your son or daughter to talk to them on your behalf or have them ask the in-law to do something.

In my situation, it is common for my wife to ask my daughters to ask their spouses about some help that I might need. When this has happened, the daughters will sometimes answer for the husband and not give him the request or chance to respond. The son-in-law may wonder why I have not asked him directly if I needed some help. I tried to make a habit of speaking directly to the sons-in-law when I want to ask for their help or information they may have.

2. Step back and take a secondary role that supports the marriage and encourages the couple to address issues they may face versus bringing these to you. Sometimes professional help can be suggested.
3. Respect the wishes, norms, and boundaries of the young-adult couple. Take the time to get to know their preferences and be respectful of these. If they like to have some notice before you come to visit, honor this. If they choose certain, different ways to celebrate special events and holidays as part of their new family traditions, honor these.
4. Be clear and firm about your wishes, values, and norms, especially as relates to them being at your home.
5. Take the lead and ask your son- or daughter-in-law for one or two suggestions of how you could be a better mother- or father-in-law. Then follow through on as many of these suggestions as you can. Maybe they will reciprocate and ask for your feedback, but don't expect it. By acting in a more caring and positive way, you will generate more positive feelings toward them. They may change as well in line with

the assumption about reciprocal relationships. Don't wait for them to change so you can have more positive feelings toward them; that doesn't work.

6. Decide on the level to which a concern or problem exists. A low-level or minor issue may best be ignored. A medium-level problem may be worth raising as a concern to determine if the other person sees it the same way. A high-level problem is something that keeps you awake at night or otherwise churning and needs to be addressed straight on.

7. When issues arise, avoid blame and seek solutions. Suppose both sets of in-laws like to have the couple over on Christmas Eve, since this has always been a tradition in their respective families. What solutions can you suggest that could respect these traditions but recognize the problem with honoring one set of parents' wishes over the other's?

8. Find common ground and ways to connect with your in-laws—shared interests, activities, events, practices, etc. Seek to build off of what you have in common.

9. Be affirming of the couple and the daughter- or son-in-law. Find positive aspects about them that you can praise and affirm.

10. Consider seeking professional help to coach and guide you on some different and more effective ways to address your concerns with in-laws. View counseling as an opportunity to get support and coaching. Family counseling may also be a consideration if all parties are willing.

Chapter 6

Grandparenting: We Never Raised Our Children Like That, and They Turned Out Okay

P arents may view the child-rearing practices of their young adult and spouse as overly indulgent, protective, or controlling, but don't believe they can provide input without offending the couple. Parents of young adults often use their own experience as the reference point for what they think their young-adult couple should do. This experience is fraught with bias and selective memories. We rewrite history and make our days with our children less stressful and more satisfying than what we experienced at the time. Parents will often comment, as my wife and I have, how they never had the level of disobedience and discipline problems their young adult parents have. Our young adults often offer a reality check to these embellished memories. As parents of these young adults, it becomes difficult not to comment or even reference our own parenting when we observe problems that our young adults are having with their children. Unfortunately, saying this can imply we did it right, and they are doing something wrong—not a good idea. My best advice is less advice—hold your tongue and offer input only if asked. Most parents know this is a good rule of thumb but find it hard to follow.

How can you influence without offending?

1. Start with accepting the reality that these grand-children are not your children. Their parents get to set the rules and expectations for the children and the grandparents. An exception is when the grand-children are visiting the grandparents, as it is appro-priate for the grandparents to establish certain guidelines and request support for these from the parents. For example, it's fair to expect the grand-children to pick up and put away all toys before they leave.
2. Approach the young adults and ask permission to offer your observations, ideas, or suggestions related to childrearing out of your experience.
3. Offer your input as a consultant. A consultant pro-vides ideas, suggestions, and guidance, but the

person to whom the consultation is offered is free to accept or incorporate some part of the advice or ignore it entirely. Start with, "Could I share my parenting experience, observations, and suggestions with you?" If offering advice, you can approach your young adult and their spouse with the following qualification before you speak: "If you choose to not incorporate any of my suggestions or ideas, I will not be offended and won't bring it up again." Keep your promise on this last point, as hard as it may be to button your lip.

4. Ask for feedback on actions that have been helpful to them as parents, as well suggestions for ways you can be helpful to them in the future.

Note: I would recommend discussing any observations and recommendations with both your young adult and their spouse. Also, if you are in a two-parent household, you should bring up the concern as a couple. If there are some aspects on which you and your spouse disagree, settle these before you present your concerns to your young-adult couple. If this face-to-face approach doesn't work or you are dismissed before you can share what you want to with them, consider writing a letter. Hand-written letters have more impact and cannot be as easily deleted or reactively responded to as a text or an email. Speak from the heart out of concern and love for them and the grandchildren. Have a good friend read this to ensure there are not subtle criticisms embedded in the comments.

Don't collude with your son or daughter in expressing concerns regarding their spouse. This puts them in an untenable, stressful position of trying to balance the concerns of their mother or father with their spouse. This act is unsupportive of the marriage and will ultimately drive a wedge between you and your young adult. This ignores the fact that as a parent to a married young adult, you are no longer number one. Accept this and be the best number two in support of the marriage you can be. A depressed client frustrated with her husband's relationship with her mother-in-law said the following:

> *"My husband chooses to listen to his mother more than me and is more willing to offend me than his mother. I'm not feeling like I am number one in his life and don't know if I can continue in this marriage unless he stands up to his mother in my defense."*

Exceptions to a Consultative Approach and/or Not Saying Anything

There are some situations where you may have to risk alienation from your young adult and spouse. Specifically, these would be situations in which the safety of the grandchildren is at risk. These can be situations of neglect, physical or sexual abuse, or parents whose lifestyles put the children at risk. In the latter case, there may be parents whose use of alcohol or other mood/mind altering substances put the children's safety at risk, or situations where there may be a mental health concern and one or the other parent is unable to be responsible. What is the guidance in these situations?

1. Out of respect for your young adult and their spouse, bring up any concern with them directly. Use the steps described earlier: "Help me solve a problem," "I am concerned," etc. It may be that they are willing to make some changes.
2. If "in person" doesn't work, bring it up with them in writing, as suggested above, and keep a copy of the letter. Share your concerns regarding the safety of the grandchildren and ask that they address these concerns either on their own or discuss these with a professional. You could indicate that you may be overreacting but would be willing to go to a family or child therapist and address these concerns, which would put your mind at ease.
3. If they are not willing to make changes or seek any professional advice and believe that you are either overreacting or misguided in your concerns, then you may need to seek professional consultation and guidance. In this regard, you should contact a child or family therapist and raise your concerns. If there is clear evidence in your reporting of neglect or risk with the grandchildren, the therapist may need to contact Child Protection. Whether or not the therapist decides to act upon the information you have shared and contacts Child Protection, you could suggest that the young-adult couple come in to respond to your concerns or discuss their parenting with a professional. In either case, there is a risk of your young adult couple becoming alienated from you out of embarrassment or a sense of betrayal, but the grandchildren's safety is at stake. If they come in

and the therapist addresses the concern, and some changes are made without the involvement of Child Protection, that's a positive outcome.

4. What if the young-adult parents are angry and decide to deny any contact with the grandchildren? Hopefully, these very sensitive situations don't lead to this, and by having you and the young adults meet with a therapist, this may be avoided.

It's so important to note that restrictions on access to grandchildren may occur for other reasons such as the young adult couple viewing the grandparents as unsafe or inappropriate with the grandchildren. A young adult shared the following concern regarding his children staying overnight with his mother.

> *"My mother has gotten drunk at times, and I have noticed that she will have wine and invite friends in when she has our kids. It makes me uncomfortable, particularly if she decided to take the children out to a store or restaurant. It's a very touchy subject, and I don't know how she would react to this."*

At times, grandparents can place grandchildren at risk and need to be respectful and responsive to the young adult's concerns. These concerns can relate to driving, use of alcohol, food that the parents have said should not be given to the grandchildren, any history of sexual or physical abuse with children, unwillingness to follow the parent's rules, excessive gift giving, and criticizing the parents or other in-laws in front of the children, to name a few. In such circumstances, the guidelines related to concerns with the young adult's parenting would apply as well. Basically, talk to the couple about their concern. Be willing to make changes that will increase the comfort and ultimately increase the access to the grandchildren. If direct efforts to address some of these don't lead to mutually agreed-upon solutions, then offer to meet with a professional to discuss the concerns and see if a third party can help mediate the situation. Grandparents do have certain rights that vary by state. Pursuing this should be a last result rather than a place to start. In fact, if seeing a therapist doesn't work, then seeking some form of mediation should be considered.

Note: Susan Forward has written a book entitled *Toxic In-Laws: Loving Strategies for Protecting Your Marriage* (2001), which is aimed at young-adult couples and their relationships with a mother- or father-in-law, that may be worth a read. Although I am not fond of stereotypes—in this case, mother- or father-in-law types—you may find yourself described in one or more of these. The best advice to young couples is in the latter part of the book, which describes strategies. Parents of young couples could benefit from reviewing these.

Enough on Reacting to Problems: Let's Talk about Being Proactive

We've been spending time dealing with problems that parents bring to my office and workshops. As a psychologist, it's easy to get pulled into this focus. But the harder and possibly more effective focus should be on preventing these problems and building a positive foundation with in-laws. Here are some positive steps you can take to build a better foundation with your young adult and in-laws.

1. Relate to your young-adult couple as you would to other adult couples. Ask for their opinions and views. Move to more of an adult-friend versus parenting role. The more you treat them as adults, the more they will act that way. A simple example is to let them pick up the tab at times when you go out to eat. The next time you are out to eat, just say, "I read in a book for parents of young adults to allow

the young adults to pick up the tab at times," and explain that you are just trying to do the right thing.

2. Treat your son- or daughter-in-law as one of the family. Family rituals, celebrations, and recurring events that have been a part of the family history need to include the son- or daughter-in-law.

3. Most in-laws feel a bit like they aren't in the in-group when the families of their spouses get together. Lots of stories shared within the family don't include the in-law, so make a special point to ask them about stories they could tell about their childhood as a way of valuing and learning more about them.

4. Make a special point of learning about and understanding the origin and value to rituals that your in-laws have had over the years. For instance, when you run into scheduling problems around holidays, be gracious and seek to find compromises. You may have to give up the expectation that your young-adult children will always be at your house on special holidays. As you have more grandchildren, you may change your mind and welcome the change of venue. The first time my wife and I went to one of our daughters' homes for Thanksgiving, it was a very nice, relaxing time.

5. Remember always to support the couple, affirm their relationship, and offer to be available to support and help them if they ask.

6. Make a point of developing a one-to-one connection with the daughter- or son-in-law. Find some common activity to share and make a point of pursuing this with them as they have time.

7. Use emails, texts, thank-you notes, or special cards to acknowledge and express appreciation of them. At different times, both of my parents have thanked my wife for being a good wife to me and mother to our children. Express pride in their accomplishments. The daughters- and sons-in-law need to know that you value them independent of their status due to marriage.

8. Respect their privacy and boundaries. They get to set boundaries of time, space, subjects of conversation (e.g. their marriage, health), etc.

9. Be careful in the use of money and avoid threats, bribes, or rewards.

10. Respect their preferences in forms of communication as well as the content. Do they want to stay connected by text or phone or face-to-face visits? When and how is it appropriate to contact them? My son will often not answer the phone when I make a call, but if I text him, he will text back—a little weird, but if that's the way he wants to connect, it's okay. He may not be able to get into a long conversation at the time but can give a quick text response. Sometimes he texts that he can't talk at the moment. That's helpful.

When I asked the parents of married young adults in my recent survey for ways to improve their relationships with their young adults, they had some helpful advice. I'm a great believer in the wisdom of the community versus just asking professionals. Take a minute to look at their suggestions, which I have listed in Appendix B.

Chapter 7

Parents: The 24/7 ATM

F inances come up as one of the specific challenges that parents face with young adults, whether single or married. It can become less of an issue when young adults marry, but there are still challenges. Facing the challenge of a young, single adult child living at home or outside the home and the question of the parent's financial involvement have been addressed in *Parenting Our Young Adults with Love and Backbone: The Practice of Supportive Integrity (2018)*, available at ParentsLettingGo.com or through Amazon. This section will be confined to discussing finances related to married or partnered young-adult children.

It's always a good practice to support the young-adult couple's independence, including their financial independence. The more the young-adult couple can "make it on their own," the stronger they will become. This is easier said than done for parents who may see their young adult and spouse struggling to make ends meet and parents have the financial capacity to help. My wife and I remember the days when we barely made it to the end of the month or rushed off to deposit a paycheck before we over-drafted. We look back with pride on making it on our own. There's something to say for getting through a tough time in life. But there may be sometimes when parents should intervene or offer to help.

First, as parents, do you have available, discretionary funds that you could tap into without jeopardizing your own quality of life or your retirement? Second, is it a need or a want on the part of the young couple? Dealing with a large medical bill is clearly a need; having a new car is not. Third, has the couple asked for help, or do you believe they would accept the help if offered? Fourth, what would be the best way to provide financial support—gift, matching grant, loan, or some in-kind contribution? On the latter point, an in-kind donation may be a car that you don't need or given at a time when you want to buy a new one. Fifth, if you are married parents of young adults, it is critical that you agree to any funding that is offered. Conditions of the funding need to be spelled out, if not in writing.

If it is an outright gift, it's important not to have strings attached or to hold the contribution over the couple's heads. Likewise, having an ulterior motive or agenda of what you want for the couple versus what they want will breed resentment and strain your relationship. At the same time, if you can offer some contribution while exploring a way they could participate and take responsibility for this, that would be helpful. In this regard, a matching grant or having the young-adult couple do some work for the parent in exchange for a cash contribution can make sense. They may feel less indebted or dependent if such an arrangement can be made. As a final check on your decision, ask yourself if your contribution will foster greater independence or dependence over the long run. If they are likely to keep asking for continued subsidy, then the contribution is likely creating more dependence.

Parents who have a lot of discretionary income and can give their young adult couple money need to be sure they are not doing this just because they can. Don't deprive your young adult couple of the chance to struggle and increase their resiliency in handling difficult circumstances including financial demands. These conditions are important to consider, but deciding when and how is not always easy.

Although parents need to make their own decision as to whether or not to fund and what to fund, here are some common areas of subsidy parents may consider:

1. Help with a down payment on a house.
2. Help with education, either of the parents or their children.
3. Help with daycare, either in-kind, taking the children x number of days a week, or providing subsidy for

childcare. A growing number of grandparents are providing some or all of the childcare services for their young-adult couple.

4. Help with unusual health insurance and excessive medical bills.

5. Contributing to a 529 educational plan for the grandchildren.

6. Funding medical or mental-health assessments or services that are not covered by insurance. Today's young couples are marrying later and having more problems getting pregnant. The costs of pursuing other options such as in vitro fertilization can be daunting to a young couple. Parents who are able and can help with these costs would be appreciated.

If the couple is having marital problems or one or the other is suffering from depression, anxiety, or other mental health-related concerns, the parents can offer to pay any out-of-pocket costs that may be incurred from obtaining these services. This takes away one of the excuses a couple might have for not pursuing counseling. It's important to note that you will not be able to have access to any information regarding the service that is delivered because this is protected under HIPPA. It is not available unless your young adult or couple signs a release. It's best not to expect a report from your young adult on progress in counseling. If they say they are not getting much out of the counseling, encourage them to discuss this with their therapist before they quit.

7. Support for vocational testing and/or coaching relative to careers or jobs can be helpful and is supportive of the young adult becoming more independent.
8. Help with some catastrophic event, which could be a medical emergency, car accident, a house burning down, etc.

The above discussion of the appropriate role of finances in parent-young adult relationships follows discussions of other issues such as in-laws, child-rearing, and some of the life stage challenges of midlife parents. In this short book, I am unable to address the many different and unique concerns that parents of young adults face in the letting-go stage that make it more complicated—such as parents or a young couple going through a divorce or the death of a family member. That said, there are some qualities of parents of young adults which, if developed and expressed, will support the letting go and growing-apart process.

Chapter 8

Do You Have the "Right Stuff" to Be a Successful Midlife Parent?

T he expression "right stuff" was popularized in a book by Thomas Wolfe in 1979 in which he refers to the qualities attributed to US test pilots. The "right stuff" refers to the qualities needed to succeed or do something well. In earlier practice books, I described several qualities parents need to have healthy, connected relationships with their young adults while successfully launching them into adulthood. These include compassion, patience, forgiveness, and empathy, among others. Let me add a few more to the list of relevance to this final letting-go stage. First, midlife parents have to **manage change**. Whether you have adult children or not, midlife is a time of change, but having adult children increases the need to change and learn new roles. It's a time to reinvest in your own personal growth as well as in the transformation of the marriage without children. This is a time to let go and grow—to find new meanings, experiences, satisfactions, and value outside the children. Being a "grower" and approaching this time as an opportunity is critical. Second, **acceptance** is a crucial quality of successful midlife parents. Daily review of the assumptions outlined at the outset of this book and recognize your inability to control or be responsible for your young adult is necessary to achieve a level of contentment and successfully launch your young adult. This is an important quality to be a grandparent and watching your young adults take different paths to raise their children. Remembering that the children are theirs not yours requires acceptance and detachment—stepping back and letting go.

Third, be a midlife parent who focuses on **gratitude** and appreciation of what you have in your children and grandchildren. Our young adults need to hear how proud we are of them, especially if they have struggled. We can affirm their persistence and commitment to succeed. Expressing gratitude and appreciation are gifts we give at no cost, but their value is beyond measure. You will never regret making the extra effort to tell our kids how much we love them and are grateful for who they are. Finally, successful midlife parents with the "right stuff" are able to **grieve**, since letting go cannot occur without this. Grieving involves saying goodbye and letting go and is a normal response to the young adult's leaving the nest. There isn't a timetable on working through this type of grief any more than the grief associated with the death of a family member. However, it's essential for both the parent and the young adult that each is able to move on with their respective lives. Reconstructing the relationship in new ways will help one move through grief. Grief should be embraced as a sign of the importance of the relationship and the joy it has brought you.

When you are sorrowful look again in your heart, and you shall see that in truth you are weeping for that which has been your delight. Khalil Gibran, *The Prophet*

Chapter 9

Time to Say Goodbye

One exercise I introduce in my workshops is to ask parents to write, and in most cases send, a letter to their young adult. Since we use the phrase "launch" to describe what we are trying to do with our young adults, I ask the parents to imagine that their young adult is leaving the country on a ship—literally launching. I ask the parents to imagine that they may never see this young adult again. In reality, from day to day, we never know if we will continue to see our loved ones—just the thought of illness and accidents can easily rob us of this assurance. What do you most want to say to your young adult as they are about to wave goodbye on their voyage to another country without a plan to return?

If you find yourself strongly resisting the idea of completing this exercise and believe that there is nothing further you need to say or your young adult needs to hear, that's fine. But please consider writing this for yourself to be able to discover and connect to those special memories and impressions you have of your young adult, as well as your hopes and dreams for them. Then after completing this, ask yourself, "Is there something I have written that my young adult really needs to hear, and am I willing to share this with them verbally, if not in writing?" In either case, I'd suggest tucking the letter or a copy of it away as something you might share later or they might find after you have passed. It would be a heartfelt gift that they would always remember. One colleague of mine who read and contributed to this book shared this story:

"I found a letter two weeks after my mom died that she had written to my two brothers and me. Although I had seen this sealed letter in my mother's jewelry box at an earlier time, I never opened it, since I could see it was something she only wanted us to read in her passing. In that letter, she shared her feelings and values she wanted us to remember. Still brings tears to my eyes, but I am so thankful she wrote it!"

Let me give you some hints or suggestions of what you might include in this letter.

1. What you most enjoyed about them as children and adolescents.
2. One or two memories that stand out about your time with them growing up.
3. Regrets you might have as a parent for which you need to apologize.
4. Actions or words you have said that you or they believe were harmful and for which you would like to ask their forgiveness.
5. Harmful actions or words for which they have apologized that you need to forgive.
6. What you wish you could do over.
7. What you have most appreciated about them as a person.
8. Ways in which they have been a blessing to you, helped you, or taught you valuable lessons.
9. What you hope for them in the future.
10. What you hope they will remember about you.
11. What you want them to know if you never see them again.
12. Other areas you wish to address in saying goodbye.

_____

_____

Sample Letter

Here is a sample letter. Not all of the questions above have been addressed, and you could certainly pick and choose the questions you would most like to answer, as well as add to the list above.

Dear Son,

I am writing to you as if you are leaving the country and I may never see you again. I know this is not happening, and I'm not planning on going anyplace either, but I just wanted to share with you my reflections on your growing-up years and my hopes and dreams for you. We all get very busy and don't take the time to share our deepest thoughts and desires, and I want you to know these.

First, I wanted to mention some things that I most enjoyed about your years growing up in our family. From the earliest of times, you were on the move. Even with a corrective device holding your two feet pointed the right way, you were able to fling yourself over the railing of the crib and escape. You were fearless in taking on a neighbor boy six inches taller than you and jumping on a two-wheel bicycle and riding it the first time without a push or help from me. Later, these athletic skills earned you opportunities to excel in high school sports, and your mother and I enjoyed watching every game you played. Now, when I drive by the little league fields and the high school, I have such fond memories of the sporting events you participated in at these sites.

Second, I wanted to say something about your character, of which I am most proud. You have always been a goal-directed and achievement-oriented individual, and this has taken you to the highest level in the medical profession. You always welcome a challenge with humility and some self-doubt, but in each case, you excel. Equally as important is your heart and openness regarding your feelings and things that have been very difficult for you. This is an unusual combination of a tough, aggressive, competitive person who excelled in contact sports in high school but could be tender and vulnerable. I will always treasure this about you.

Third, I have tried to reflect on any regrets I have had about you or our relationship, and I don't have many. You might have a few of which you could remind me, and I would welcome these and an opportunity to apologize. Two incidents stand out. I remember holding your younger sister when you came up and persisted at bugging me about something you wanted, even after I said no. So I did a leg sweep while I was sitting down and knocked your legs out from under you.

It didn't hurt you, but I saw a stunned look on your face. I am not sure you will even remember it, but I was ashamed at what I had done. Please forgive me. On another occasion, I got really mad and verbally berated you. I remember coming out of the dry cleaner's after picking up my clothes, and you were in the car and made some condescending remark that just set me off; I verbally let you have it. Again, afterward, I was very ashamed of this and knew that I overreacted. I don't remember that I apologized to you, but please accept my apology now.

Fourth, I have pondered the question of what I would do over in raising you, and I don't have an immediate answer to this. I know I was quite busy and could clearly have given more time to you and could have done more things with you outside of attending sporting events. I do have some fond memories of traveling to Duluth or your maiden voyage to the Casino in Hinckley as part of your learning to drive and prepare for your license. Those were great times of just being together with you. As adults, we have had some more times like that of backpacking and sailing together that are such good memories.

Fifth, I have many hopes for you, some of which have already come true—being married and fathering two boys. I never envisioned you going into the medical field but am so very proud of the hard work you put into becoming a physician and the pride you have in your work. Along with the goal-directed and achievement side of you, there is a very conscientious side of wanting to do the best you can as a physician and provide your patients the very best care they could get.

My hopes for the future are that you will have a long and fulfilling marriage and family life and achieve all of what you want in life. At the same time, I want to encourage you to not abandon your caring, sensitive, and vulnerable side. I also can't help but encourage you to continue to be a seeker of answers to life's deeper mysteries and questions.

Sixth, when I look back on my life, I hope you will remember me in some particular ways. I want you to remember me as always loving you deeply and unconditionally. Don't ever doubt my love for you. I would also like to be remembered as a person of integrity who was true to his word, faithful to his marriage, and committed to his family. In general, I would like to be remembered not as an exceptional person in any special way, but just as a good and honorable person of whom you can be proud to call your dad.

Life is so very short, and good times become memories so quickly that we don't have time to savor them. All the more reason to take this time to savor the relationship that I had and have with you and how proud I am to call you son. Thanks for the taking the time to read this, and don't feel obligated to respond in any way.

With love and affection,

Dad

Chapter 10

Doing Your Own Report Card

E ach day is one more day of saying goodbye. As each day passes, we have to look in the mirror and ask ourselves how we did as a parent. Did we reach the standards that we set for ourselves? If we depend on the judgment of others regarding our parenting, we put our good feelings about ourselves at risk. A common theme in the practice books that I have written is the idea of doing your own report card. By this, I mean identifying what you need to do to be the best parent you can be at this midlife stage. If we give our report card to our young adults, we give up our power and put our self-esteem at risk. Should their opinion matter? Absolutely. But at the end of the day, we can't control what other's think—including, and especially, our young-adult children.

I'll offer a couple suggestions for the report card, but please, list what you think is important. Once completed, focus on and review these actions daily or weekly. At the end of the day or week, identify where you have done well and where you could improve and recommit to both areas. Share your report card with your spouse, partner, or friend and ask them to listen, ask questions, and challenge you if they think you may be grading yourself too hard or too easy. The question you ask when you look in the mirror is not, "Have I pleased my young adult or anyone else?" but, "Have I been the best parent I could be today or last week?"

My Report Card

Date:___/___/___

My Intended Improvement Actions	My Actual Action	My Grade	My Plan
Actions motivated by love			
Actions consistent with my principles			
Actions supportive of my young adult's independence			

Chapter 11

Take Action

W hat actions will you take as a result of reading this book and committing to being a more effective parent at this stage of your young adult's life? Experience suggests that if you don't take at least one action in the next twenty-four hours, you will likely not follow through on any good intentions you have of applying what you have learned. For some, just committing to discussing key learnings and possible changes, or creating your report card, in the next twenty-four hours with your partner, a close friend, or even your young adult could be an important first step.

In the next twenty-four hours, I will:

_____

_____

_____

_____

Chapter 12

Keepers

W ith each book, I try to pull out what I believe are important "keepers," tips or suggestions to keep in mind from reading this book. Please feel free to come up with your own list of keepers because your list may be different than mine. Here's mine:

1. Take the time to be sure you are listening to, connecting with, and understanding your young adult, and their spouse if they are married. Understanding is always the starting point.

2. Communicate your unconditional love for your young adult and how much they matter to you and extend this to their spouse. Practice loving actions toward your son- or daughter-in-law; it will soften your heart and theirs.

3. Say goodbye, let go, and start to grow apart, unless you are still emotionally entangled with your young adult due to feelings of anger, resentment, guilt, fear, or anxiety. If these exist, revisit the need to apologize and forgive, which are addressed in earlier practice books.

4. Be aware of challenges such as empty nest, sandwich generation, and a midlife crisis that are creating stress and need to be addressed apart from your relationship with your young adult.

5. If your young adult is single, treat them as an adult and be clear about what you will do and won't do to help them with their launch.

6. Approach the empty nest stage as a time of transformation and new opportunities—a time to transform your marriage and your relationship with your young adult, and a time for new experiences, new friendships, and new additions to the family.

7. Approach midlife as a time to reinvest in yourself, your health, and your wellbeing; reflect and turn inward to find new and deeper purposes for the second half of your life.

8. Expand the concept of family to include in-laws and grandchildren and invest in these new relationships with a commitment to build positive and lasting bonds. Be the best grandparent you can be.

9. Balance your own needs for privacy, time alone, or your marriage with clear communications of what you can give to your young-adult couple in regarding time, presence, and help—financial and otherwise.

10. Reform your relationship with your young adult or young-adult couple to be a good friend, offer consultation, or advise, especially when asked, but with the qualification that they are always expected to make their own decisions.

Appendix A

Advice to couples in the empty-nest phase of the family life cycle, from a survey conducted in May 2018 with twenty parents of young-adult couples.

Prepare for it by taking more time with each other in advance.	Establish a dating culture; pray together regarding the transition.
Explore new hobbies, careers, or passions.	Remember what brought you together and renew your relationship.
Be patient, relax, and don't be too hard on yourselves.	Don't act out of your neediness.
Prepare and plan for the empty nest.	Give your spouse space; don't try to meet all of your needs through your spouse.
Stay in touch with the children while enjoying the freedom.	Enjoy the possibilities and don't look back.
Let the children figure things out before jumping in.	Make a list of dreams and compare notes.
Spend quality time together.	Be open to innovation, creativity, play, detachment, and imperfection.
There's a lot of letting go.	Develop friends at a similar stage of life.
Everyone should look for joy in this phase of their lives; be grateful.	Find a balance with your spouse with each having interests outside the home.
Work things out; discuss difficulties and love one another.	Enjoy grandchildren; they are wonderful.

Appendix B

Parents' suggestions for improving the relationship with your adult child and spouse, from a survey conducted in May 2018 with twenty-five parents of married young adults.

Act only as a consultant, not an adviser.	Be transparent and vulnerable.
Give them the freedom to fail or succeed—to make their own mistakes.	Ask for their preferred method of contact.
Be a good listener; listen nonjudgmentally.	Let go of expectations.
Don't try to control them.	Wait to be invited; don't intrude.
Recognize their accomplishments.	Communicate without judgment.
Accept, connect with, and build up your spouse.	Show interest in them.
Hear what they didn't like about their childhood.	Ask for forgiveness for past failures.
Help them become financially independent.	Always be willing to help.
Initiate time and conversation with them.	Treat them with respect and expect they treat you likewise.
Be honest with yourself about your shortcomings.	Avoid criticism, especially of mistakes they make.
Be supportive and let them know you love them.	Don't take it personally when they spend time with other parents.
Accept their independence.	Be involved.
Keep communication lines open, always.	Treat them equally.

Be sure to support and include the spouse.	Respect their boundaries.
Never issue an ultimatum.	Don't let pride get in the way.
Honor their parenting style.	Recognize it is a privilege and not a right to have a say in their lives.

Notes

1. John Stoltzfus, *Differentiations and Delinquent Youth* (Ann Arbor, Michigan: University Microfilms International Print Copy, 1982).
2. Doug Flagler, "Parenting Advice regrets from Empty Nesters," Posted April 16, 2018. https://fox13now.com/2018/04/16/parenting-advice-and-regrets-from-empty-nesters.
3. K. Parker and E. Patten, *The Sandwich Generation: rising financial burdens for middle-aged Americans* (Pew Research Center, 2013).
4. Jeffrey Jensen Arnett and Joseph Schwab, "The Clark University Poll of Parents of Emerging Adults," Clark University, Worcester, Massachusetts, September 2013.
5. Google Survey Link, https://www.think-withgoogle.com/data-gallery/detail/millennial-parents-child-best-friends/
6. Fusion Poll, https://fusiondotnet.files.wordpress.com/2015/02/parents.pdf
7. Macaela MacKenzie, "The Average Age of Marriage Right Now," Women's Health, (March 26, 2018).
8. Madeleine A. Fugere, "Why You and Your Mother-in-Law May Not Get Along," https://www.psychology today.com/us/blog/dating-and-mating/201610/why-you-and-your-mother-in-law-may-not-get-along.

9. Terri Apter, *What Do You Want from Me?* (New York and London: W.W. Norton and Company, 2009).

Bibliography

Arnett, Jeffrey Jensen and Tanner, Jennifer Lyn. *Emerging Adults in America: Coming of Age in the 21st Century.* Washington D.C. American Psychological Association. 2006.

Carter, Betty and Monica McGoldrick. *The Expanded Family Life Cycle: Individual, Family and Social Perspectives.* Third Edition. Boston, Mass. Pearson Education Company, 2005.

Casey, Karen. *Letting Go: Embracing Detachment.* San Francisco: Conari Press, 2010.

Coleman, Joshua. *When Parents Hurt.* New York: William Morrow, 2008.

Forward, Susan. *Toxic In-Laws: Loving Strategies for Protecting Your Marriage.* New York: Harper Collins Books, 2001.

Gibran, Kahlil. *The Prophet.* New York: Alfred A. Knopf, Inc. 1923.

Lesser, Elizabeth. *Broken Open: How Difficult Times Can Help Us Grow.* New York: Villard, 2005.

Seigel, Daniel. *Mindsight: The New Science of Personal Transformation.* New York: Bantam Books, 2011.

Five Practice Books by Jack Stoltzfus available at ParentsLettinGo.com and Amazon:

Stoltzfus, John. *Can You Speak Millennial "ese"?: How to Understand and Communicate with Our Young Adult.* Shoreview, Minnesota: Self Published, 2017.

Stoltzfus, John. *Love to Let Go: Loving Our Kids Into Adulthood.* Shoreview, Minnesota: Self Published, 2017.

Stoltzfus, John. *Apology: The Gift We Give Our Young Adults.* Shoreview, Minnesota: Self Published, 2017

Stoltzfus, John. *Forgiveness: The Gift We Share with Our Young Adults.* Shoreview, Minnesota: Self Published, 2017.

Stoltzfus, John. *Parenting Our Young Adults with Love and Backbone: The Practice of Supportive Integrity (2018)* Shoreview, Minnesota: Self Published, 2018.

CPSIA information can be obtained
at www.ICGtesting.com
Printed in the USA
LVHW021048300619
622776LV00014B/418

9 781545 660065